at the
BEACH

Written by

MELANIE CUDNIK, M.S., CCC-SLP
and LAUREN PADULA, M.S., CCC-SLP, ATP

at the
BEACH

Written by
MELANIE CUDNIK, M.S., CCC-SLP
and LAUREN PADULA, M.S.,CCC-SLP, ATP

Meet Abby and Cole.
Abby is curious, kind, and full of big ideas. Cole is clever, brave, and has a lot to say. Cole communicates in a special way—he uses augmentative and alternative communication, or AAC to share his thoughts, ask questions, and join in the fun.

And Abby? She's right there with him every step of the way—listening, encouraging, and helping Cole grow his language superpowers!

So come along! There's a whole world to discover with Abby, Cole, and the power of AAC!

"What a lovely day it is outside!" Abby said with a smile, looking out the window as she waited for Cole to reply.

Cole joyfully used his talker to let Abby know where he wanted to spend the day. "Go beach."

Abby thought it would be a wonderful idea to go to the beach. She turned to Cole with a big smile and said, "The beach is pretty!"

"We are going to the beach! I hear birds. I hear waves. They sound like music!" Abby feels so happy. Cole pressed his talker and says, 'Like music.' Abby smiles.
Like music.
LIKE
MUSIC
MUSIC

This reminded Abby of a song.

Let's GO to the beach, let's see what we find,
Seashells and crabs, Oh, what a good time! With
the sun shining bright, and the breeze in our hair.
C'mon let's GO, the beach is right there!

Go shells..
GO
shells
GO
BEACH
shells

Abby smiled. "Find shells? GO!" she said
with a laugh.
She began to look all around the beach,
searching for shells big and small.

Shell go up.

Abby looked ahead and saw a tall sandcastle shining in the sun.
"Wow!" she said. "Why don't we put this pink shell on this beautiful sandcastle?"

Cole looked at his device and tapped, "shell go up."
Abby laughed. "Yes! The shell goes up on the castle!"

SHELL
GO
UP
GO
DOWN

Where shell go?
WHERE
shell
GO
GO
BEACH
shell

Cole looked at the castle and couldn't see the shell.
He tapped his device, "Where shell go?"

Abby looked down and smiled. "Oh! The shell fell off. Here it is — in the sand!"

She picked it up and put it back on the castle.

Abby noticed something moving in the distance, her eyes lighting up with excitement. She exclaimed, "Hey, check that out! I think I see something! Could that be a dolphin?"

Abby and Cole enjoyed a fantastic day at the beach, filled with laughter and fun. "So, where shall we head next, Cole? I'm starting to feel quite hungry," she said.

Sometimes it's in the everyday moments — like commenting, wondering, and sharing excitement — that real language growth happens. Throughout this story, Abby modeled rich language by commenting, expanding on Cole's messages, and responding naturally.

Whether they're building rocket ships, exploring jungle trails, or solving mysteries in their backyard, Abby and Cole show that communication comes in many forms — and that every voice matters.

EXPANDING LANGUAGE SKILLS

Receptive Language

Where did Cole want to go?

What color was the shell that Abby and Cole found?

Who saw the dolphin first?

Expressive Language

What is your favorite thing to do at the beach?

What was your favorite part of the story?

AAC tip

Draw and describe. Have the student draw events of the story, and then use their AAC device to describe what's happening in the picture.

To view Abby and Cole in action, and to hear the Go to the Beach song, be sure to visit our YouTube channel.

About The Authors

Melanie Cudnik, M.S., CCC-SLP

Melanie is a Speech-Language Pathologist with over a decade of experience diagnosing and treating children with a wide range of communication needs—from nonverbal communicators to those with language and articulation disorders. She is certified in Gestalt Language Processing and is passionate about helping each child find their voice through creativity, connection, and play. With a creative eye, a love of storytelling, and a deep appreciation for music that she incorporates into her therapy sessions, Melanie brings language to life through engaging visuals, rhythm, and everyday adventures. She believes communication grows best through joyful, child-led moments—where curiosity sparks confidence and every voice is valued.

Lauren is the Owner and Lead Clinician of TechAbilities Consulting, LLC, based in New Jersey. She is a licensed Speech-Language Pathologist, a certified Assistive Technology Professional (ATP) through RESNA, and a certified Autism Spectrum Disorder Clinical Specialist (ASDCS), bringing more than 15 years of experience to the field. Lauren specializes in a neurodiverse-affirming approach to Augmentative and Alternative Communication (AAC) and assistive technology, supporting individuals in accessing their fullest potential through innovative tools and strategies. Guided by the belief to "access the possibilities with Assistive Technology," Lauren is dedicated to inspiring communication, learning, and independence for individuals of all abilities.

Lauren Padula, M.S., CCC-SLP ATP